by Iain Gray

PUBLISHING

WRITING *to* REMEMBER

LangSyne

PUBLISHING

WRITING *to* REMEMBER

79 Main Street, Newtongrange,
Midlothian EH22 4NA
Tel: 0131 344 0414   Fax: 0845 075 6085
E-mail: info@lang-syne.co.uk
www.langsyneshop.co.uk

Design by Dorothy Meikle
Printed by Printwell Ltd
© Lang Syne Publishers Ltd 2017

ISBN 978-1-85217-515-3

Griffiths

MOTTO:
The good times will come
(and)
Strength and health.

CREST:
A demi-lion rampant.

NAME variations include:
Griffith
Griffin
Gruffudd *(Welsh)*

Chapter one:

The origins of popular surnames

by George Forbes and Iain Gray

If you don't know where you came from, you won't know where you're going is a frequently quoted observation and one that has a particular resonance today when there has been a marked upsurge in interest in genealogy, with increasing numbers of people curious to trace their family roots.

Main sources for genealogical research include census returns and official records of births, marriages and deaths – and the key to unlocking the detail they contain is obviously a family surname, one that has been 'inherited' and passed from generation to generation.

No matter our station in life, we all have a surname – but it was not until about the middle of the fourteenth century that the practice of being identified by a particular surname became commonly established throughout the British Isles.

Previous to this, it was normal for a person to be identified through the use of only a forename.

But as population gradually increased and there were many more people with the same forename, surnames were adopted to distinguish one person, or community, from another.

Many common English surnames are patronymic in origin, meaning they stem from the forename of one's father – with 'Johnson,' for example, indicating 'son of John.'

It was the Normans, in the wake of their eleventh century conquest of Anglo-Saxon England, a pivotal moment in the nation's history, who first brought surnames into usage – although it was a gradual process.

For the Normans, these were names initially based on the title of their estates, local villages and chateaux in France to distinguish and identify these landholdings.

Such grand descriptions also helped enhance the prestige of these warlords and generally glorify their lofty positions high above the humble serfs slaving away below in the pecking order who had only single names, often with Biblical connotations as in Pierre and Jacques.

The only descriptive distinctions among the peasantry concerned their occupations, like 'Pierre the swineherd' or 'Jacques the ferryman.'

Roots of surnames that came into usage in England not only included Norman-French, but also Old French, Old Norse, Old English, Middle English, German, Latin, Greek, Hebrew and the Gaelic languages of the Celts.

The Normans themselves were originally Vikings, or 'Northmen', who raided, colonised and eventually settled down around the French coastline.

The had sailed up the Seine in their longboats in 900AD under their ferocious leader Rollo and ruled the roost in north eastern France before sailing over to conquer England in 1066 under Duke William of Normandy – better known to posterity as William the Conqueror, or King William I of England.

Granted lands in the newly-conquered England, some of their descendants later acquired territories in Wales, Scotland and Ireland – taking not only their own surnames, but also the practice of adopting a surname, with them.

But it was in England where Norman rule and custom first impacted, particularly in relation to the adoption of surnames.

This is reflected in the famous *Domesday Book*, a massive survey of much of England and Wales, ordered by William I, to determine who owned what, what it was worth and therefore how much they were liable to pay in taxes to the voracious Royal Exchequer.

Completed in 1086 and now held in the National Archives in Kew, London, 'Domesday' was an Old English word meaning 'Day of Judgement.'

This was because, in the words of one contemporary chronicler, "its decisions, like those of the Last Judgement, are unalterable."

It had been a requirement of all those English landholders – from the richest to the poorest – that they identify themselves for the purposes of the survey and for future reference by means of a surname.

This is why the *Domesday Book*, although written in Latin as was the practice for several centuries with both civic and ecclesiastical records, is an invaluable source for the early appearance of a wide range of English surnames.

Several of these names were coined in connection with occupations.

These include Baker and Smith, while Cooks, Chamberlains, Constables and Porters were to be found carrying out duties in large medieval households.

The church's influence can be found in names such as Bishop, Friar and Monk while the popular name of Bennett derives from the late fifth to mid-sixth century Saint Benedict, founder of the Benedictine order of monks.

The early medical profession is represented by Barber, while businessmen produced names that include Merchant and Sellers.

Down at the village watermill, the names that cropped up included Millar/Miller, Walker and Fuller, while other self-explanatory trades included Cooper, Tailor, Mason and Wright.

Even the scenery was utilised as in Moor, Hill, Wood and Forrest – while the hunt and the chase supplied names that include Hunter, Falconer, Fowler and Fox.

Colours are also a source of popular surnames, as in Black, Brown, Gray/Grey, Green and White, and would have denoted the colour of the clothing the person habitually wore or, apart from the obvious exception of 'Green', one's hair colouring or even complexion.

The surname Red developed into Reid, while

Blue was rare and no-one wanted to be associated with yellow.

Rather self-important individuals took surnames that include Goodman and Wiseman, while physical attributes crept into surnames such as Small and Little.

Many families proudly boast the heraldic device known as a Coat of Arms, as featured on our front cover.

The central motif of the Coat of Arms would originally have been what was borne on the shield of a warrior to distinguish himself from others on the battlefield.

Not featured on the Coat of Arms, but highlighted on page three, is the family motto and related crest – with the latter frequently different from the central motif.

Adding further variety to the rich cultural heritage that is represented by surnames is the appearance in recent times in lists of the 100 most common names found in England of ones that include Khan, Patel and Singh – names that have proud roots in the vast sub-continent of India.

Echoes of a far distant past can still be found in our surnames and they can be borne with pride in commemoration of our forebears.

Chapter two:

Freedom fighters

Although ranked 57th in some lists of the 100 most common surnames in England, 'Griffiths' has from earliest times been particularly identified with Wales.

It is derived from the Welsh personal names 'Gruffin', 'Griffith' and 'Griffin' – all forms of 'Gruffudd' – while the ancestors of those who would later come to bear it as a surname were present in Wales pre-dating the arrival on British shores of invaders such as the Romans, Vikings, Anglo-Saxons and Normans.

This means that flowing through the veins of many bearers of the Griffiths name today is the blood of the ancient Britons.

Of Celtic pedigree, these early inhabitants of the British Isles were settled for centuries from a line south of the River Forth in Scotland all the way down to the south coast of England and with a particular presence in Wales.

Speaking a Celtic language known as Brythonic, they boasted a glorious culture that flourished even after the Roman invasion of Britain in 43 AD and the subsequent consolidation of Roman power by about 84 AD.

With many of the original Britons absorbing aspects of Roman culture, they became 'Romano-British' – while still retaining their own proud Celtic heritage.

Following the withdrawal of the last Roman legions from Britain in 406, what is now modern-day Wales, or *Cymru*, fragmented into a number of independent kingdoms – with the most powerful king being recognised as overall ruler.

Regarded as King of the Britons, he had to battle with not only internal rivals but also the depredations of the wild sea rovers known as the Vikings, or Northmen.

There were also the Anglo-Saxons to contend with – as those Germanic tribes who invaded and settled in the south and east of the island of Britain from about the early fifth century were known.

These Anglo-Saxons were composed of the Jutes, from the area of the Jutland Peninsula in modern Denmark, the Saxons from Lower Saxony, in modern Germany and the Angles from the Angeln area of Germany.

It was the Angles who gave the name 'Engla land', or 'Aengla land' – better known as 'England.'

The Anglo-Saxons held sway in what became England from approximately 550 to 1066, with the main kingdoms those of Sussex, Wessex, Northumbria, Mercia, Kent, East Anglia and Essex.

Whoever controlled the most powerful of these kingdoms was tacitly recognised as overall 'king' – one of the most noted being Alfred the Great, King of Wessex from 871 to 899.

The Anglo-Saxons, meanwhile, had usurped the power of the indigenous Britons, such as those found in Wales, and who referred to them as 'Saeson' or 'Saxones.'

It is from this that the Scottish Gaelic term for 'English people' of 'Sasannach' derives, the Irish Gaelic 'Sasanach' and the Welsh 'Saeson.'

The death knell of Anglo-Saxon supremacy and also what remained of Welsh independence was sounded with the Norman Conquest and the defeat of Harold II, the last of the Anglo-Saxon monarchs, at the battle of Hastings.

Within an astonishingly short space of time, Norman manners, customs and law were imposed on

England – laying the basis for what subsequently became established 'English' custom and practice.

One famous ancestor of some who would later adopt the Griffiths name was the ninth century Rhodri the Great, known in Welsh as Rhodri Mawr or Rhodri ap Merfyn.

Born in about 820, Rhodri was the first to rule most of what would become present-day Wales.

Inheriting the kingdom of Gwynedd on the death of his father in 844, he went on to gain the other powerful kingdoms of Powys and Seisyllwg – but he faced twin threats from the Vikings and the Anglo-Saxons.

Victorious in battle over the Vikings in 865, killing their leader Gorm, he had to flee for a time to Ireland after losing in battle to them twenty years later on Anglesey.

Back in his native Wales a year later, both he and his son Gwriad were killed in battle in 878 against the Anglo-Saxon Ceolwulf II of Mercia.

It is through one of his descendants, Gruffudd ap Cynan that bearers of the Griffiths name today can proudly trace a descent from this founder of what is known as the first royal tribe of Wales.

Born in about 1055, he became a prominent

figure in the bitter Welsh resistance to Norman rule and, after years of bloody struggle, eventually became established as King of Gwynedd.

A freedom fighter much in the same mould as the great Scottish warrior William Wallace, he gained a number of glorious victories over the Normans in addition to suffering a number of devastating defeats.

Captured in 1081 by the Norman Hugh, Earl of Chester and Hugh, Earl of Shrewsbury at Rug, near Corwen, after being betrayed by one of his own men, he was imprisoned for about twelve years in the Earl of Chester's castle.

Escaping from confinement thanks to a bold and fearless character known as Cynwrig the Tall who, after taking advantage of Cynan's captors being distracted while attending a feast, he went on to regain control of Welsh territories from the Normans.

The first to be honoured with the title of Prince of Wales, he died in 1137, while his son Owain Gwynedd and his great-grandson Llewellyn the Great – known in Welsh as Llyweln ap Iorwerth and described as 'head and king and defender and pacifier of all Wales' – continued fierce and dogged resistance to Norman rule.

In 1282, by which time most of Wales had come under Anglo-Norman rule, final rebellion against this was crushed by England's Edward I, and it is from this date that the heir apparent to the British throne has borne the title of Prince of Wales.

An abortive rebellion was led in the early fifteenth century by the freedom fighter Owain Glyndŵr, while in the following century, under Henry VIII, Wales was 'incorporated' into the English kingdom.

In 1707, in common with Scotland, Wales became part of the United Kingdom.

Chapter three:

Politics and pictures

The Griffiths name is one that features prominently in the historical record of not only its original heartland of Wales but also in those of other nations.

Born in 1792 at Glanmeilwch, Carmarthenshire, David Griffiths was the Welsh Christian missionary who has the distinction of having been among the first to translate the Bible into an African language.

A member of the Congregational Church, it was after studying at its missionary college at Gosport and being ordained as a minister that he and his wife, Mary, embarked for Madagascar in 1820.

Establishing a church and a school, in addition to preaching he also translated the Bible into the Malagasy language, making its teachings accessible for the first time to the country's Christian adherents.

Returning to Britain in 1842 and acting as pastor of the Congregational Church at Hay-on-Wye, Powys, he died in 1863 after having completed a revised Malagasy translation of the Bible.

Not only an eminent Egyptologist but also a

prominent Welsh political activist and poet, John Gwyn Griffiths was born in 1911 in Porth, in the Rhondda Valley.

A graduate in Latin, Greek and Egyptian studies, he qualified as a teacher in 1934, while from 1936 to 1937 he served as an archaeological assistant with the Egyptian Exploration Society at Sesesi, Lower Nubia.

The author of a number of important works on Egyptian religion, he was married to the German-born Käte Bosse-Griffiths, a fellow scholar in Egyptology who became keeper of archaeology at Swansea Museum.

A conscientious objector during the Second World War, he worked for a time as a teacher before, in 1959, being appointed to a senior lectureship at Swansea University and, in 1965, as a reader in classics.

In 1946, meanwhile, he and his wife started editing the Welsh-language magazine *Y Flam – The Flame* – while he also became closely involved with the national party for Wales known as Plaid Genedlaethol Cymru, known today as Plaid Cymru.

A key figure in the promotion of Welsh language in both education and law and having written a number of acclaimed Welsh language poems, he died in 2004.

Another noted Welsh poet was David Rees Griffiths, born in 1882 and who died in 1953 and whose Bardic, or Celtic poetic name, was Amanwy.

He was a brother of the Welsh trade union leader and early twentieth century Labour Party politician James Griffiths – the first ever Secretary of State for Wales.

Better known as Jim Griffiths, he was born in 1890 in the village of Betws, near Ammanford, Carmarthenshire, the son of a blacksmith and the youngest of ten children.

His rise through the ranks of trade unionism and mainstream politics was as impressive as it was meteoric.

Leaving school aged only 13 to work in a local coal mine, he furthered his education by attending night school and, despite being wearied after a hard day's toil, burning the midnight oil to study on his own.

Establishing a branch of the Independent Labour Party in Ammanford in 1908, he became its secretary, while from 1916 to 1919 he held the post of secretary to the Ammanford Trades Council.

Thanks to a miners' scholarship, he was able to leave the mines in 1919 to study at the Central Labour College, London.

Returning to his native Wales, he worked as a Labour Party agent from 1922 to 1925 and then, from 1934 to 1936, in the powerful post of President of the Miners Federation of South Wales.

Elected Labour Member of Parliament (MP) for Llanelli in 1936, he was elected three years later to the party's national executive committee, while following Labour's victory in the 1945 General Election he was made a Privy Councillor and Minister for National Insurance.

It was in this role, along with fellow Welsh Labour Party politician Aneurin Bevan, that he became one of the main architects of Britain's Welfare State – introducing pioneering legislation that included the Family Allowances Act of 1945, the National Insurance Act of 1948 and an Industrial Injuries Act.

Appointed in 1964 by Labour Prime Minister Harold Wilson as the first Secretary of State for Wales, Griffiths was responsible for the establishment of the Welsh Office.

Appointed a Companion of Honour, he remained in Parliament until five years before his death in 1975, author of the autobiographical *Pages from Memory*.

Another noted Welsh bearer of the proud name of Griffiths was the celebrated photojournalist Philip Griffiths, known for his coverage of the Vietnam War.

Born in 1936 in Rhuddlan, the son of a transport company supervisor and a district nurse, he studied pharmacy and worked for a time in London in a branch of a pharmacy chain before obtaining employment as a part-time photographer for the *Manchester Guardian* newspaper.

Hired as a freelance photographer for the *Observer* newspaper in 1961, he covered France's bitter conflict in Algeria in 1962 while in 1966 he arrived in war-torn Vietnam as a photographer for the *Magnum* picture agency.

His early photographs of the war, concentrating on the suffering of the ordinary Vietnamese people, proved difficult for *Magnum* to sell to American magazines – which at the time tended to shy away from the reality of what was rapidly becoming a horrifying conflict.

But Griffiths was able to continue his coverage of the war, his pictures beginning to find a more receptive audience among Americans who were questioning their nation's role in the conflict.

Published in 1971, his celebrated *Vietnam Inc.* book illustrated with his photographs and detailing the horrors of the conflict from the side of the Vietnamese and serving U.S. soldiers and regarded now as a classic in photojournalism, further galvanised public opinion against the war.

Later covering the Yom Kippur War between Israel and Egypt in 1973 and working in Cambodia from 1973 to 1975, he was appointed president of *Magnum* in 1980, serving in the post until 1985.

The author of other works that include his collection *Dark Odyssey* and *Agent Orange*, he died in 2008.

One bearer of the Griffiths name with a rather unusual claim to photographic fame was Frances Griffiths who, along with her cousin Elsie Wright, claimed to have photographed fairies at the bottom of Elsie's garden.

It may well sound fanciful, but many prominent figures of the day, including Sherlock Holmes' author Sir Arthur Conan Doyle, were convinced as to the authenticity of the pictures.

In what is known as the tale of the *Cottingley*

Fairies, it was in the summer of 1917 that ten-year-old Frances Griffiths and her mother arrived from South Africa to live for a time with Frances' aunt, sixteen-year-old Elsie's mother, at their home in the village of Cottingley, West Yorkshire.

The cousins regularly played together at a small stream at the bottom of the garden and, scolded by Elsie's mother for coming back with wet feet and clothes, they told her they had been there 'to see the fairies.'

Elsie's father was a keen amateur photographer, and to prove their point about the existence of the fairies, the cousins borrowed his camera.

One day, they excitedly rushed in to tell him they had photographed the fairies and, when Elsie's father developed the photographic plates, he discerned an image of Frances behind a bush in the foreground on which tiny fairies were dancing.

Further photographs followed over the next few days, including one of Elsie holding out her hand to a 1ft. tall gnome – but, suspicious from the outset, her father dismissed it all as a childish prank.

There matters may have rested until Elsie's mother attended a meeting in Bradford of the Theosophical Society for a lecture on "Fairy Life."

At the end of the meeting she showed her daughter and niece's photographs to the speaker and the affair then rapidly began to take on a life of its own.

Through the speaker, the pictures came to the attention of leading members of the society – who believed in a cycle of evolution for humanity towards increasing perfection.

They then came to the attention of Sir Arthur Conan Doyle who, as a firm believer in spiritualism, was convinced they were evidence of psychic phenomena and used them to illustrate an article he had written on fairies for a 1920 edition of *The Strand Magazine*.

Interest in the *Cottingley Fairies* gradually waned until, in 1966, a photographer for the *Daily Express* newspaper managed to track down Elsie Wright – who claimed that what may have occurred was that she and Frances may have 'photographed their own thoughts.'

But before their deaths in the 1980s, both Elsie and Frances finally admitted that the photographs had been faked – using cardboard cut-outs of fairies copied from *The Princess Mary's Gift Book*, which had been a popular children's book of their time.

Intriguingly, however, Frances insisted that although they had faked photographs, one of them was genuine.

Francis Griffiths died in 1986 and Elsie Wright two years later, while the original glass photographic plates of the *Cottingley Fairies* were sold at auction in 2001 for £6,000.

Other material relating to them, including a letter written by Elsie admitting the hoax, is now held in the National Media Museum, Bradford.

Chapter four:

On the world stage

Bearers of the Griffiths name and their namesakes of Griffith have gained international recognition through a wide range of pursuits.

Born in Melbourne in 1968, **Rachel Griffiths** is the award-winning Australian actress of television and film whose first major screen credit was the 1994 *Muriel's Wedding*, while four years later she was nominated for an Academy Award for Best Supporting Actress in *Hilary and Jackie*.

Television credits include the series *Six Feet Under* and *Brothers and Sisters*, for which she was nominated for a Golden Globe Award for Best Supporting Actress.

Other big screen credits include the 2006 *Step Up*, the 2009 *Beautiful Kate* – for which she received an Australian Film Institute Award for Best Actress in a Supporting Role – and the 2011 *Burning Man*.

Born in 1957 in New York City, **Melanie Griffith** is the American actress who was the recipient of an Academy Award for Best Actress for her role of Tess McGill in the 1988 *Working Girl*.

The role also won her a Golden Globe Award for Best Actress, Motion Picture Musical or Comedy, while other big screen credits include the 1984 *Body Double*, the 1997 *Lolita* and the 2005 *Heartless*.

The daughter of the actress Tippi Hedren and the late film producer Peter Griffith, she has been married since 1996 to the actor Antonio Banderas.

A leading British character actress, **Lucy Griffiths**, born in 1919 in Birley, Hertfordshire is best known for her roles in a number of Hammer House of Horror films.

These include the 1960 *The Two Faces of Dr Jekyll* and the 1974 *Frankenstein and the Monster from Hell*, while other film credits include a number of *Carry On* comedy films such as *Carry on Constable* and *Carry on Behind*. Also with television credits that include *On the Buses*, *All Creatures Great and Small*, *Z-Cars* and *Secret Army*, she died in 1982.

Her namesake, **Lucy Griffiths**, is the contemporary English actress best known for her role of Maid Marian in the popular 2006 to 2009 television series *Robin Hood*. Born in 1986 in Brighton, her other television credits include *Sea of Souls*, *Sugar Rush*, *Lewis* and *True Blood*.

An acclaimed Welsh actor of stage, television

and film, **Hugh Griffith** was born in 1912 in Marianglas, Anglesey. Studying at the Royal Academy of Dramatic Arts, London up until the outbreak of the Second World War when he served in India and in the Burma Campaign, he took to the stage again in 1946.

Starring in 1952 beside fellow Welsh actor Richard Burton in a Broadway production of *Legend of Lovers*, six years later both he and the actor Anthony Perkins were nominated for a Tony Award for Best Actor for their roles in the Broadway production *Look Homeward, Angel*.

On the big screen, his major credits include the 1959 *Ben-Hur*, for which he won the Academy Award for Best Supporting Actor, the 1963 *Tom Jones*, for which he received an Academy Award nomination, the 1965 *The Amorous Adventures of Moll Flanders* and the 1979 *A Nightingale Sang in Berkeley Square*.

Also with television credits that include *Quatermass II* and the 1978 comedy series *Grand Slam*, he died in 1980.

The daughter of the British actors Annette Crosbie and Michael Griffiths, **Selina Griffiths** is the actress born in 1969 in Richmond upon Thames, Surrey. Popular television series in which she has appeared include *Drop the Dead Donkey*, *The Smoking*

Room, *Benidorm*, *Being Human* and the BBC costume drama *Cranford*.

The recipient of an OBE for his services to the acting profession, **Richard Griffiths** was the actor of stage and screen born in 1947 in Thornaby-on-Tees, Yorkshire. The son of a steelworker, it was after studying at what is now the Manchester School of Theatre that he worked for a time with the Royal Shakespeare Company.

The recipient of several awards for his role in the stage production of *The History Boys* that included a Tony Award for Best Performance by a Leading Actor in a Play, he died in 2013.

His major screen credits include the role of Vernon Dursley in the *Harry Potter* series of films, the 1980 *Superman II*, the 1982 *Ghandi* and the 2006 film of *The History Boys*, while his many television credits include *Pie in the Sky*, *Bergerac*, *Inspector Morse* and the 2012 *The Hollow Crown – Henry V*.

Born in Manchester in 1983, **Ciarán Griffiths** is the English actor best known for his roles of Mickey Maguire in the television series *Shameless* and as Gary Best in *The Bill*. Other television credits include *Coronation Street*, *Clocking Off* and *Waterloo Road*, while big screen credits include the 2007 *The Visitor*.

Behind the camera lens, **Howard Griffiths**, born in 1935 in Swansea and who died in 1999, was the screenwriter whose film credits include the 1965 *Licensed to Kill* and, after immigrating to Australia, a number of television series that include *Hunter* and the police dramas *Blue Heeled*, *Division 4* and *Homicide*.

Bearers of the Griffiths name have also excelled in the highly competitive world of sport.

On the green baize of the snooker table, **Terry Griffiths** is the Welsh retired champion born in Llanelli in 1947. Working in a variety of jobs that included postman, insurance salesman, coal miner and bus conductor, he won the Welsh Amateur Championship in 1975 and the English Amateur Championship in 1977 and 1978 – the year he turned professional.

He went on to win the World Championship in 1979, the Masters in 1980 and the UK Championship in 1982; this made him one of only seven players to date to have completed snooker's Triple Crown.

Retiring from professional play in 1997, he has since coached top players who include Mark Williams, Ali Carter and Stephen Hendry, while he also commentates on the game for the BBC.

From snooker to athletics, **Cecil Griffiths**, born in Neath in 1901, was the Welsh runner who was a gold medal winner at the 1920 Olympics as a member of his country's 4x400-metres relay team.

Also the winner of the British AAA (Amateur Athletics Association) championship in 1923 and 1925 in the 800-yards event, he died in 1945.

In the wrestling ring, Barri Griffiths, born in 1982 in Tremadog, is the Welsh professional wrestler better known by his ring name of **Mason Ryan** and as "Goliath" – the name under which he appeared in the 2009 series of the television show *Gladiators*.

On the fields of European football, **Leigh Griffiths**, born in 1990 in Leith, Edinburgh is the talented Scottish striker who has played for teams that include Livingston, Dundee, Wolverhampton Wanderers and Hibernian; he has also played for the Scotland Under -19, Under -21 and B Teams.

Born in Cardiff in 1980, **Rhys Griffiths** is the striker who has played for teams that include Cwbran Town, Carmarthen Town and Plymouth Argyle; a seven-time winner of the Welsh Premier League Golden Boot Award, at the time of writing he is the second highest goal scorer in the history of the league.

In the creative world of art, **David Griffiths**, born in Liverpool in 1939 but moving to Wales with his family when he was aged seven, is the portrait painter whose many acclaimed works include his portrait of Prince Charles on the occasion of his investiture as Prince of Wales in 1969.

In the world of music, Jemma Griffiths, better known as **Jem**, is the Welsh singer and songwriter born in 1975 in Penarth. Best-selling albums include her 2004 *Finally Woken* and the 2008 *Down to Earth*, while international hit singles include her 2005 *It's Amazing* and the 2009 I *Want You To* …

Known as the "Queen of Reggae", **Marcia Griffiths** is the female singer of bands that have included Bob and Marcia and the I Threes, who were a back-up group for Bob Marley and the Wailers.

Born in 1949 in Kingston, Jamaica, her 1976 *Electric Boogie*, re-released in 1989, became the music for a line dance and is the biggest-selling single of all time by a female reggae singer.

Born in 1953 in Seguin, Texas, **Nanci Griffith** is the American singer, songwriter and guitarist whose 1993 *Other Voices, Other Rooms* won a Grammy Award for Best Contemporary Folk Album, while other best-selling albums include her 1989 *Storms* and the 2002 *Winter Marquee*.

One particularly enterprising bearer of the proud name of Griffiths was the Welsh farmer and businessman **Robert Griffiths**. With the business philosophy of 'explore all markets, pinpoint the best, and gear all production to exploit it', he became a successful dairy farmer and producer of a range of dairy produce, with contracts that included selling cream to the upmarket Harrods store in London.

Born in Montgomeryshire in 1886, he began in the dairy business during the First World War after renting a farm at Garthllwyd. By the 1950s, he had bought the Woodlands farm at Forden, Powys, in addition to the 2,000-acre Walcot Estate near Lydbury North.

A partner in one of the first artificial insemination companies in the United Kingdom, in 1961 he won the prestigious Sir Bryner James Memorial Award of the Royal Welsh Agricultural Society for his exceptional contribution to dairy farming in Wales.

Another lucrative business venture was the founding in 1933 of Direct TT Supplies, set up to market his milk and other products directly to the public through a number of popular Milk Bars in his native Wales and in the north of England.

Appointed High Sheriff of Montgomeryshire in 1953, before his death in 1962 he was awarded the honour of Commander of the Most Venerable Order of the Hospital of St John of Jerusalem.